BALI TRAVEL
2023-2024

The Updated Travel Information To Explore The Beautiful Bali Island,Beach And Culture

Greg.P. Moyer

TABLE OF CONTENT

INTRODUCTION

Welcome to Bali, a tropical paradise and one of the most enchanting destinations in Indonesia! This island is renowned for its stunning beaches, rich culture, and lush landscapes, attracting travelers from all corners of the globe. Whether you're seeking relaxation on pristine shores, immersing yourself in Balinese traditions, exploring ancient temples, or indulging in local cuisine, Bali offers an unforgettable experience for every type of adventurer.

In this comprehensive Bali travel guide, we'll equip you with everything you need to know to make the most of your trip to this magical island. We'll delve into Bali's history, culture, and the top attractions you shouldn't miss. We'll also provide practical tips on transportation, accommodation options, and navigating the diverse neighborhoods of Bali.

Bali has a captivating history that dates back centuries. Once a prominent center for trade and culture, the island boasts a unique blend of Hindu traditions and local customs. From ancient temples adorned with intricate carvings to vibrant festivals that celebrate Balinese heritage, you'll find a cultural richness that permeates every corner of the island.

One of the iconic landmarks you can't miss in Bali is the majestic Tanah Lot Temple. Perched on a rocky islet amidst crashing waves, this temple offers breathtaking sunset views and a glimpse into Bali's spiritual side. You'll also be awestruck by the intricate architecture and serene atmosphere of Uluwatu Temple, situated on a cliff overlooking the Indian Ocean.

For nature lovers, Bali's lush landscapes and picturesque rice terraces are a treat for the senses. Head to Tegalalang Rice Terrace or Jatiluwih Rice Terrace to witness the magnificent beauty of Bali's agricultural heritage.

The island is famous for its sandy beaches, and you'll be spoiled for choice when it comes to sun-soaked retreats. Whether you prefer the lively atmosphere of Kuta Beach, the tranquil shores of Nusa Dua, or the surfer's haven of Uluwatu Beach, there's a perfect spot for everyone.

When in Bali, a visit to the Ubud Monkey Forest is a must. This sanctuary is home to playful monkeys and ancient temples, offering a unique experience with nature and culture.

Bali's arts and crafts scene is also vibrant, with traditional dance performances, skilled artisans, and bustling markets. Make sure to catch a Barong dance or visit local craft villages like Celuk for silver jewelry and Mas for wood carvings.

Getting around Bali is convenient, with a variety of transportation options. Taxis, motorbike rentals, and ride-sharing services are readily available. For longer journeys, hiring a private driver or using shuttle services are popular choices.

Accommodation in Bali caters to all budgets and preferences. Whether you're looking for luxurious beachfront resorts, cozy boutique hotels, or budget-friendly hostels, you'll find plenty of options. Popular areas to stay include Seminyak, Ubud, Canggu, and Nusa Dua, each offering a distinct atmosphere.

Each neighborhood in Bali exudes its own charm and allure. Seminyak is known for its trendy beach clubs and high-end shopping, while Ubud is the cultural heart with its art galleries and lush surroundings. Canggu attracts a younger crowd with its hip cafes and surf culture, and Nusa Dua is perfect for a relaxed beach getaway.

In this travel guide, we'll provide detailed insights into all of Bali's top attractions, along with tips to maximize your experience. From navigating local customs to enjoying traditional cuisine, we'll ensure you have an unforgettable and enriching journey on this captivating island.

Whether you're a first-time visitor or a seasoned traveler, welcome to Bali! Embrace the beauty, hospitality, and spirituality of this island paradise, and we hope you have an incredible stay in this enchanting destination.

ABOUT THIS GUIDE

Welcome to the travel guide to Bali, Indonesia. This comprehensive guide has been crafted to help you make the most of your visit to this enchanting island paradise. We've gathered all the essential information you'll need to plan your trip, providing recommendations on where to stay, what to see and do, and how to get around.

In this guide, you'll discover information on all the major attractions in Bali, as well as some hidden gems that are waiting to be explored. We'll also equip you with practical tips and advice, from transportation options to dining choices, to ensure you navigate the island like a seasoned traveler.

Bali offers a rich tapestry of experiences, catering to history enthusiasts, culture aficionados, adventure seekers, and those seeking pure relaxation. Whether you wish to delve into ancient temples, witness traditional ceremonies, surf the waves, or unwind on pristine beaches, this guide has something for everyone. We've carefully curated content covering the vibrant areas of Kuta, Seminyak, Ubud, and more, so you can fully immerse yourself in the diverse wonders of Bali.

Get ready to embark on a journey of discovery, as you delve into the breathtaking landscapes, vibrant culture, and warm hospitality that Bali has to offer. Let this guide be your companion as you create unforgettable memories during your visit to the Island of the Gods.

CHAPTER 1

GETTING TO KNOW BALI

Undoubtedly, the most well-known tourist destination in Indonesia is the Island of the Gods. It embodies the ideal tropical paradise. The hotels, taverns, and restaurants on the island receive daily tiny offerings of flowers and burning incense sticks. The passing of a procession of Balinese wearing white robes is announced by the soft gong sound. For the past several hundred years, visitors to the island have been enchanted by this rich culture.

The southern towns and beaches of Bali are the main tourist attractions. Young party goers are drawn to Kuta, while hipsters frequent Canggu, yogis congregate in Ubud, the young and wealthy prefer Seminyak, and all-inclusive 5-star resorts can be found in Nusa Dua. This diversity makes Bali such a simple pick for a restful vacation.

As soon as you leave the city behind, you are surrounded by hills covered in dense forests and rice fields. The routes take you past sleepy towns and solitary temples nestled on hillside slopes—the ideal setting for a cycling journey. Numerous gushing waterfalls where you can swim can be found in the highlands, and they all flow into raging rivers where white water rafting is popular. You could even go canyoning and spend the day abseiling and jumping over waterfalls if you're feeling very daring.

East Java, rather than Yogyakarta, is where you should go to see Java's stunning landscapes. The majority of tourists travel in a 3-Day, 2-night package from Surabaya or Malang to Bromo and then the Ijen Volcano. If you have time, add it to your schedule.

GEOGRAPHY AND CLIMATE

Geography of Bali

One of Indonesia's provinces, Bali Island is situated halfway between Java Island and Lombok Island. The frame area of this island is bounded by the Indian Ocean in the south, the Lombok Strait in the east, the Laut Bali (Bali Sea) in the north, and Bali Strait in the west. There are five islands that make up the 5.632,86-square-kilometer Bali Province: Bali Island, Nusa Penida Island, Nusa Lembongan Island, Nusa Ceningan Island, and Menjangan Island. Bali is divided into 8 districts, 53 sub districts, and 674 villages, according to the administration.

THE LOCATION OF BALI ISLAND

Geographical Location of Bali - The island of Bali is located 8 degrees south of the equator, 3.2 kilometers (2 miles) east of Java. The Bali Strait divides Bali from Java. The island's land area is 5,632 km2, and it is approximately 153 km (95 mi) wide from east to west and 112 km (69 mi) long from north to south.Several peaks in Bali's central mountains rise above 3,000 meters. The "mother mountain" and active volcano, Mount Agung (3,031 m), is the one in question.

Mount Agung is the easternmost summit in a group of mountains that extend from the center to the eastern side. The significant rainfall Bali receives from its lofty mountain ranges and volcanic soil has helped to contribute to the island's unparalleled fertility. The majority of Bali's substantial rice production is grown in a vast, progressively dropping plain south of the mountains. The primary coffee-producing region of the island is on the northern side of the highlands, which also produces rice, vegetables, and cattle. The Ayung River, which is the longest river, flows for about 75 km.

Reefs of coral surround the island. While beaches in the north and west often have black sand, those in the south typically have white sand. Although small sampan boats can travel the Ho River, Bali lacks significant rivers. Apart from Tanah Lot's beachfront temples, the black sand beaches between Pasut and Klatingdukuh are being developed for tourism, but they are not yet heavily utilized.

Near the southern coast, Denpasar, the provincial capital, is the major city. In 2002, it had about 491,500 residents. The former colonial capital of Bali, Singaraja, which is on the north coast and has a population of about 100,000, is the island's second-largest city. Other significant cities include Kuta, a beach resort that effectively forms part of Denpasar's urban area, and Ubud, the island's cultural hub, which is located to the north of Denpasar.

Nusa Penida, Nusa Lembongan, and Nusa Ceningan are three tiny islands located immediately to the south-east of Bali and are all administratively a part of the Klungkung regency of Bali. Badung divides these islands from Bali.

The biogeographical boundary between the fauna of the Indo-Malay ecozone and the significantly different fauna of Australasia is marked by the Lombok Strait, which divides Bali from Lombok to the east. After Alfred Russel Wallace, who initially suggested a transition zone between these two important biomes, the transition is known as the Wallace Line. Bali shared the Asian flora with Java, Sumatra, and the Asian mainland when sea levels plummeted during the Pleistocene ice age, but Lombok and the Lesser Sunda archipelago remained separated due to the deep waters of the Lombok Strait.

Due to its role in facilitating travel between Java and other islands in Bali Island's eastern region (Nusa Tenggara), Bali Island is an important location. Bali is situated halfway between Australia and Asia. Agung Mount (3.142 meters), Gunung Batur (1.717

meters), Abang Mount (2.152 meters), and Batukaru Mount (2.276 meters) are some of the mountains that are geographically located in the heart of Bali.

Aside from mountains, Bali also contains a few lakes, including Tamblingan Lake (110 Ha), Buyan Lake (336 Ha), Beratan Lake (375,6 Ha), and Batur Lake (1.605 Ha). Bali Island is located in a tropical region that experiences the Dry Season and the Wet Season twice a year. The humidity is about 79%, and the temperature ranges between 24,0° C to 30,8° C.

CHAPTER 2

TRIP PLANNING

BEST TIME TO VISIT BALI

The dry season on the island, which lasts from April to October, is the ideal time to visit Bali. The island experiences some soupy, humid days throughout the year, while having excellent weather for travelers. Restaurants are less crowded during the mid-season months, and many stores have sales and promotions. You can expect to see luxuriant raindrops, cloudy skies, and heavy clouds that are ready to release rain. The island experiences powerful wind gusts between June and August. The sight of hundreds of Balinese kites dancing in the wind is something that is very lovely about this time of year, and why shouldn't it be? As the Balinese people refer to it, it is "kite season" at the moment. Bali is busiest at this time of year.

Bali's busiest months are July, August, and December.
Christmas-New Year and July-August are two of the busiest times of year in Bali, whether spending time on a busy beach or mingling with festive throngs of people appeals to you. A delightful mix of rain and dry weather, with sporadic showers and lengthy bright days, can be found throughout July and August. Bali has luxuriant showers and an increase of about 90 mm in rainfall during the winter.

Bali's shoulder season (February, May, June, and October–December)
Enjoy wonderful weather and lower costs during shoulder season. Even though there is a lot of activity on the streets, they are not packed. You'll discover that it's frequently possible to see famous temples, buildings, and other tourist attractions without having to worry about crowded crowds.

Bali slows down to a calm simmer in the first three months of the year after the revelry of New Years and Christmas. In Bali's low season, it rains unrepentantly, so if you decide to venture outside, you'll frequently require an umbrella or raincoat. But there are plenty of reasons to begin the year in Bali, including lower hotel rates and fewer tourists.

THE CLIMATE OF BALI

Dry Season: April To October

Average temperature: 27 degrees Celsius at the low, 31 degrees Celsius at the high.

Weather: The dry season in Bali is a huge draw for tourists from around the world. Large numbers of foreign visitors flock to Bali during the dry season due to the pleasant weather. Australia's warm, dry air is carried by southeast winds to Bali's warm coasts. You've never seen sky this blue, and the air is crisp. The sea is ideal for all types of adventure water activities as the warm, sunny weather of the day cools down to colder temperatures in the nights. The humidity is also minimal. The best weather for visiting Bali is when you catch the perfect curl of the wave when surfing or dive into the ocean to discover a coral kingdom.

Significant occurrences: With the entrance of the strong southeast winds, Bali begins preparing with a kite for the annual Kite Festival, which takes place between July and August. Don't miss the Ubud Food Festival if you're in Bali in April, when the season is just getting started. Attend the Nusa Dali Blues festival in June (you'll hear about it before you see it); it's a big music festival in Bali with a lot of local and foreign bands. Take a break from flying kites in July to check out the Bali Art Festival, and join the natives in celebrating Bali's Independence Day in August.

Reasons to go right away:You may create the ultimate holiday by combining ideal weather, several festivals, and the ideal beach wave.

Even though it's the dry season, you should still prepare for rain or showers by packing an umbrella and sunblock.

During this season, book your lodgings and tickets in advance. You could find products to be more expensive because the dry season is so well-liked by travelers.

Wet Season: November through March

Average temperature: 27 degrees Celsius in the peak and 25 degrees Celsius in the low

Bali's wet season is characterized by steamy and slightly sticky weather. Bali's rainy season is marked by overcast, gloomy skies, rougher surf, and a shift in the island's mood from joyful and celebratory (during the Christmas-New Year holiday season) to calm and reflective (in January and February). Due to lower prices and more manageable crowds, this time of year is preferred by many tourists. This island may have heavy rain from December through February. There are alternative activities like canyoning and white water rafting that thrill-seeking tourists can participate in despite the unappealing state of the beaches.

Even though there may be fewer tourists in Bali this season, the island is nonetheless bustling with events and activities for both residents and visitors. In Jembrana, West Bali, November marks the Makepung Buffalo Races. Add the Denpasar festival to your Christmas and New Year's celebration schedule because December is a month of intense festivity. The months of January, February, and March are generally quieter, but the month of March will take things to a whole new level of stillness since that month is Nyepi Day, when everyone in the area observes silence and refrains from using any light.

Reasons to go right away:Rainy days make for a lovely island, and you'll also have many tourist attractions to yourself since Bali is less popular at this time of year.

Consider this before you go: Try to avoid making this a beach trip! Bali's wet season weather makes the sea excessively turbulent, and the leftovers from Christmas and New Year's festivities typically leave the beaches filthy.

Tips:For a stress-free spa day, substitute the beach!

VISA AND ENTRY REQUIREMENTS

1. Validity of Passport: Everyone visiting Bali must have a passport that is valid for at least six months beyond the day they want to depart. Before making trip plans, confirm that your passport satisfies this criteria.

2. Visa Exemptions: a. Visa-Free Entry: People from a wide range of nations are not required to obtain a visa in order to visit Bali for up to 30 days for tourism. The United States, Canada, the United Kingdom, Australia, New Zealand, the majority of the members of the European Union, and numerous more nations are among those that qualify. For the most recent information, it is advised to contact the Indonesian embassy or consulate in your country as the availability and terms of visa-free access may vary.

a. Visa on Arrival (VoA): If you are from a nation that is not permitted to enter without a visa, you can receive a Visa on Arrival when you arrive in Bali. The VoA permits stays of up to 30 days, which can be doubled up for another 30 days. It's vital to check your eligibility in advance because visas-on-arrival are not available for all nationalities.

3. Visa Extensions: The local immigration office in Bali can help you get a visa extension if you want to extend your stay past the initial visa-free or Visa on Arrival term. It is advised to begin the extension procedure at least a week before your visa is set to expire. In most cases, extensions are valid for an extra 30 days.

4. Social/Cultural Visa: Travelers who intend to stay in Bali for longer lengths of time, such as for study, volunteer work, or cultural exchange programs, may submit an application for a Social/Cultural Visa at an Indonesian embassy or consulate in their place of residence. This visa permits a stay of up to 60 days at first, with a total of four 30-day extensions available.

5. Multiple Entry Business Visa: Travelers on business may apply for a Multiple Entry Business Visa (MEBV) if they must enter Indonesia frequently for work-related reasons. With each stay being limited to 60 days, this visa allows repeated entries during

a calendar year. A corporation from Indonesia is required to sponsor the MEBV.

6. Visa Requirements: The following documents are normally required for the majority of visa types:
completed visa application form.
b. A current passport that is good for at least six months.
c. Recently taken photos the size of a passport.
d. Documentation of a subsequent or return trip.
a. Enough money on hand to cover your hotel bill.
f. Information on lodging options or documentation of a hotel reservation.
g. Extra documentation relevant to the type of visa (such as a letter of sponsorship or an invitation).

TRANSPORTATION ALTERNATIVES

The Indonesian island of Bali, a well-known tourist destination, has a variety of ways to move around. You may want to think about the following popular transportation options:

Especially in the well-known tourist locales like Kuta, Seminyak, and Ubud, taxis are widely available in Bali. Taxis can be ordered using ride-hailing applications like Grab or Gojek or by flagging one down on the street.

Apps for ride-hailing: Grab and Gojek are two prominent ride-hailing services in Bali, as was already noted. Cars, motorcycles, and even food delivery are among the convenient and reasonably priced mobility options they provide.

Private Drivers: One popular method of discovering Bali is by hiring a private driver. For a half-day or full-day rental, you can haggle a price, and the driver will transport you wherever you want to go as well as to various sights. Your itinerary can then be more flexible and individualized as a result.

Scooter and car rentals: If you want the flexibility to explore the island at your own leisure, renting a scooter or car is another popular option. In Bali, there are numerous automobile rental companies, so if you intend to drive, it's a good idea to have a valid international license.

Renting a bicycle is an option for getting around in various regions, including Ubud and Canggu. It's an excellent way to get to know the surrounding areas, especially if you like to move slowly and take in the landscape.

Public Buses: The public bus service in Bali is rather limited. It mostly connects some tourist hotspots and serves the major towns. The schedules, however, could be erratic, and the buses might fill up quickly. It's not the most practical choice, but on some routes it can be more cost-effective.

Motorbike Taxis: Also referred to as "ojeks," motorcycle taxis are a common and reasonably priced form of transportation, particularly for short trips. You can haggle the price before getting on because they are typically easily accessible.

Depending on where you are staying and the distance you need to travel, walking may be a pleasant alternative. Particularly in more condensed regions like Ubud, it's a terrific opportunity to experience the local vibe.

When selecting your means of transportation in Bali, keep things like the flow of traffic, the safety of the roads, and your comfort in mind.

ACCOMMODATION OPTIONS

INFORMATION YOU MUST KNOW BEFORE BOOKING A BALI HOLIDAY

Do I book a room in a hotel, resort, or villa?

There are a variety of accommodations available in Bali, ranging from modest guesthouses (Losmen) maintained privately-serviced by welcoming Balinese families to opulent beach resorts and beachfront villas with a driver and a kitchen. The cost of lodging is comparable, and you'll be astounded by Bali's renowned high quality of customer care and employee friendliness.

Where should I stay in Bali?

Decide where in Bali you want to stay before deciding on the precise type of lodging; this is just as crucial, if not more so.

Travelers can immerse themselves in the vibrant social scene in the touristy parts or enjoy a luxurious hideaway in one of the boutique hotels, peaceful private villas, or vacation rental homes that can also be found in the island's more secluded regions. Even in the more well-known regions, backpackers will be pleasantly surprised by the nice, comfortable lodging that is affordable. On practically any part of the island, those who choose luxury can do it for a very affordable price while living like a king or queen.

LOCATIONS

Therefore, we strongly advise you to familiarize yourself with Bali's primary DESTINATIONS before moving further and looking for your accommodation. In fact, Bali has many diverse places to visit. Changing locations every four to five days and exploring different locales while on vacation is a favorite pastime for many tourists. We would also advise visitors to Bali to do that. Knowing which of the more than a dozen various places in Bali best suit your needs and preferences is crucial.

To accommodate every taste and budget, Bali provides a wide selection of lodging options:

Luxury Resorts and Villas: Pamper yourself in one of Bali's top-notch resorts, or book a private villa with breath-taking vistas and first-rate amenities.

Boutique Hotels: The lovely boutique hotels dispersed over the island offer individual attention and distinctive lodging.

CHAPTER 3

TOP BALI ATTRACTIONS

Ubud, the center of Bali's culture

The mood, surroundings, and climate of Ubud, a town recognized as the cultural center of Bali, contribute to a sense of well-being that may be savored.Ubud is actually made up of fourteen villages, each of which is managed by a separate banjar (village council), despite the fact that it looks to outsiders to be a one tiny town.Along the rivers are terraced rice fields, and distant from the town center, ordinary village life goes on with little disruption. Tourists abound and the center of Ubud is extensively commercialized.

The history of Ubud may be traced back to the eighth century. The area was a hub for alternative medicine and healing at the time, and this is where the term Ubud came from:

Balinese medicine dates back thousands of years and is called Ubad.

Architectural remnants from this time period include the Gunung Kawi temple complex and the cave temples in Goa Gajah. This is when a lot of the rituals, dances, and plays that are still performed in Ubud today got their start.

The colonialists did not meddle much when Ubud was made a Dutch protectorate in 1900 at its own request, which allowed the region's traditional arts and cultures to survive largely unaltered.

The royal family encouraged international artists to establish presences in the town in the 1930s, which marked the start of Ubud's modern era. Travelers first began to arrive in the 1960s, mainly adventurous types because the infrastructure was still quite rudimentary.

The town stretches out in all directions for many kilometers, and "Ubud" is a broad term that refers to all of the minor settlements that are located within five kilometers of the major market. It is manageable to go around on foot if you pick a lodging option that is relatively central.

The most important historical sites are situated outside of town, some up to 20 kilometers away.

In the northern section of the village is the Pura Puseh Batuan Temple, a historic building from the 11th century that is adorned with beautiful stone carvings. It is a five-tiered entrance tower that is definitely inspired by Indian temple architecture. However, it has characteristic Balinese iconography and decorations. A Bhoma head that looks over the main doorway is one of the notable representations.

An elaborately carved demon's mouth serves as the entrance to the ninth-century cave known as Goa Gajah (Elephant Cave). There are some shattered lingam and yoni figurines within, along with a Ganesha statue. A small walk leads to a waterfall, rice fields, and some Buddhist stupa remnants, and large, carved guards protect pools close to the entrance. The Goa Gajah complex was not completely excavated until the 1950s. Compared to other places of interest near Ubud, this location is somewhat unimpressive.

The eleventh-century Pura Gunung Kawi (Poet Mountain Temple), which is located at the bottom of a narrow valley surrounded by rice fields and is accessible by 371 stairs, is a beautiful structure. It's difficult to up all those steps, but it's worth it to see one of Bali's largest and oldest ancient monuments in this verdant river valley. The buildings are cut into the sides of a narrow river valley, which is itself traversed by winding vines and trees. Before entering the main pura complex, you must take off your shoes.

There are other tomb cloisters around a kilometer downstream.

The 11-tiered meru in the inner courtyard of Pura Kehen, also known as the Kehen Temple, which was built in 1206, is particularly remarkable. Up until the 1940s, Puri Saren Agung (also known as the Royal Palace or Water Palace) served as the residence of the kings of Ubud, and some royal descendants still reside there.

Tirta Empul and Tampaksiring. One of Bali's holiest temples built around hot springs that still bubble in the center courtyard. The sacred barong masks are bathed here during Galungan, and the Balinese come here to bathe and cleanse themselves physically and spiritually. The spring's water is pure and reputed to have mystical properties.

The Tegenungan Waterfall

Of course, one must also go to the Monkey Forest in Ubud. Not only are the monkeys friendly and won't bother you like they may elsewhere, but the stroll and surroundings are also quite enjoyable.

Kuta and Seminyak: Beaches and Nightlife

Bali, Indonesia, is home to two well-known tourist destinations: Kuta and Seminyak. They are renowned for their stunning beaches and exciting nightlife. The nightlife and beaches of Kuta and Seminyak are described below:

Beaches:

- Kuta Beach: Kuta Beach is one of Bali's most well-known beaches and spans for several kilometers along the west coast. It offers gorgeous sunsets, smooth white beach, and excellent surf breaks. Swimming, tanning, and other water sports like bodyboarding and surfing are all popular on the beach.

- Seminyak Beach: This stunning coastline is immediately to the north of Kuta Beach. In comparison to Kuta, it is somewhat quieter and has a more affluent vibe. The beach is well-known for its upscale hotels, beach clubs, and hip beachfront bars. Seminyak Beach is a terrific place for leisurely stroll along the shoreline and also offers breathtaking sunsets.

Nightlife:

- Kuta Nightlife: Kuta is renowned for its exciting and dynamic nightlife scene. There are many bars, nightclubs, and live music establishments lining the main thoroughfare, Jalan Legian. It's a well-liked location for partygoers, especially for younger tourists. Sky Garden, Bounty Discotheque, and Paddy's Pub are a few of Kuta's well-known nightlife destinations.

- Seminyak Nightlife: In comparison to Kuta, Seminyak provides a more affluent and upmarket nightlife experience.

Numerous swanky bars, up-and-coming nightclubs, and beach clubs may be found nearby. A lively environment is created in Seminyak's beach clubs because of the numerous DJs who spin music all day and all night. Potato Head Beach Club, Ku De Ta, and La Favela are a few places in Seminyak with a thriving nightlife.

In terms of beaches and nightlife, Kuta and Seminyak both accommodate a variety of tastes. While Seminyak provides a more premium and sophisticated experience, Kuta is more lively and dynamic. For a sense of the distinctive vibes that each location has to offer, visitors to Bali frequently like seeing both locations.

Tanah Lot Temple - Stunning Ocean Views

For its breathtaking ocean views, Tanah Lot Temple is well recognized. One of Bali, Indonesia's most well-liked tourist destinations, it is. Near the seaside, the temple is perched atop a rocky outcrop, giving the impression that it is floating on the ocean during high tide.

The Balinese term "Tanah Lot" translates to "Land in the Sea" Hinduism in Bali accords tremendous prominence to the temple, which is devoted to the sea goddess Dewa Baruna. The temple complex, which features numerous shrines, pavilions, and exquisitely planted gardens, is open to visitors.

In addition to the temple itself, the breathtaking surroundings include the rocky shoreline and the roaring waves against it. Especially around dusk when the temple is illuminated by a warm golden light, the expansive ocean vistas from Tanah Lot Temple are quite beautiful.

To capture the magnificent surroundings of the temple, photographers and nature lovers frequently throng to Tanah Lot. In addition, there are a number of viewpoints and dedicated viewing sites where guests can take in the temple and the ocean from various perspectives.

It's crucial to remember that Tanah Lot Temple can get very crowded due to its popularity, particularly during the busiest travel seasons. The breathtaking ocean vistas and distinctive cultural experience make it a must-visit location for many visitors to Bali.

Mount Batur Volcano and Sunrise Trek

Bali, Indonesia is home to the active volcano Mount Batur. Known for its breathtaking sunrise views and difficult trekking options, it is a well-liked travel destination for adventure seekers.

Usually starting in the Baturearly morning hours to witness the sunrise, the trek to the top of Mount is a unique experience. Guided trekking packages to Mount Batur are widely available from Bali's tour companies, and they normally include breakfast, transportation, and a local guide.

Depending on your level of fitness, the hike itself normally takes two to three hours. For most persons with a basic level of fitness, it is a moderate hike. Although the trail is well-marked and generally secure, some parts of it can be difficult and rough.

The Toya Bungkah settlement, which is at the mountain's base, is where the trek often begins. Using the tour company-provided flashlights, you will start your ascent from there in the pitch-black. Your local guide will lead you around the volcanic scenery while pointing out noteworthy points and watching out for your safety.

The trek's ultimate objective is to ascend Mount Batur before sunrise. The spectacular panoramic views of the surrounding mountains, Lake Batur, and the faraway ocean will be your reward once you've reached the top. Awe-inspiring is an understatement when describing the morning view from this vantage point.

You may tour the crater after taking in the sunrise and get a close-up look at the steam vents and volcanic activity. The walk will have a greater educational component thanks to the guide's explanations on the geology and history of the volcano.

You'll start your descent back to the starting point once you've had enough time to explore the summit. Visits to Toya Bungkah's natural hot springs are a part of certain trips; here, you can unwind and soak in the therapeutic waters to revive your achy muscles.

Booking with a reliable tour operator who offers knowledgeable guides and takes safety precautions seriously is advised if you are thinking about making the climb to Mount Batur. Carry enough water, wear layers of clothing to accommodate shifting temperatures, and wear comfortable trekking shoes.

Overall, the Mount Batur sunrise climb is an amazing experience that combines physical exertion, scenic beauty, and a breathtaking sunrise vista. For those who enjoy the outdoors and the great outdoors, Bali is the place to go.

Uluwatu Temple: Cliffside Temple and Kecak Dance

On Bali, Indonesia's southwest coast, stands Uluwatu Temple, also known as Pura Luhur Uluwatu, a well-known Hindu temple. It offers wonderful panoramic views of the ocean and magnificent sunsets as it perches on a cliff about 70 meters above the Indian Ocean.

It is devoted to the spirits of the sea and is one of Bali's six main spiritual pillars. The island is thought to be shielded from any evil spirits that might emerge from the sea by this belief. For its distinctive design and spectacular location, Uluwatu Temple is well-known.

The Kecak Dance performances at Uluwatu Temple are well-known, in addition to its natural beauty. In the 1930s, the Kecak Dance, a traditional Balinese dance and music theater, first appeared. A huge number of men sit in a circle and act out various characters from the Hindu epic Ramayana while chanting "cak" in a rhythmic manner.

The dance usually takes place in the amphitheater of the temple or on a nearby stage at dusk, adding to the enchanted atmosphere. The play portrays the tale of Prince Rama's struggle to save his wife Sita from the control of the evil king Ravana. A group of musicians and singers perform alongside the dancers, who are dressed in traditional attire.

The fascinating Kecak Dance performance and the Uluwatu Temple's cliffside setting together provide tourists to Bali a singular and unforgettable cultural experience. To get a good place to appreciate the temple and the dance while taking in the spectacular views, it is advised to get there early.

Tegallalang Rice Terraces - Stunning Scenery

The Tegallalang Rice Terraces are a wonderful site with picturesque scenery. These rice terraces are a well-known representation of the island's natural beauty and are situated in the town of Tegallalang in Ubud, Bali, Indonesia. Here is a description of the stunning beauty found at the Tegallalang Rice Terraces:

The Tegallalang Rice Terraces are a series of cascading tiers of vivid green rice paddies that have been carved into the contours of the steep environment. These terraces represent an ancient agricultural heritage that Balinese farmers have passed down through the years and show how cultivation and nature can coexist together.

The complex irrigation system known as "subak" will captivate you as you explore the terraces. The subak system allows for a controlled flow of water from springs and rivers to the rice fields, preserving the ideal conditions for rice cultivation. It is quite beautiful to see the water flowing through the terraces as it glistens in the sunlight.

When the light bathes the environment during the golden hours of sunrise or sunset, a warm and ethereal mood is created, the terraces provide spectacular panoramic views. Photographers and nature lovers can't help but be drawn in by the dramatic contrast created by the interplay of light and shadow across the stacked rice paddies.

The Tegallalang Rice Terraces have gained popularity as a tourism destination in addition to their agricultural significance, drawing tourists from all over the world. Visitors may get a close-up view of the agricultural miracle by strolling along the curvy roads that wind through the terraces.

Many of these routes lead to quaint roadside cafes and shops where you can sip a cool coconut or buy regional crafts.

Be sure to bring your camera if you want to capture the stunning Tegallalang Rice Terraces. The terraces provide a plethora of photo opportunities, whether you want to document the expansive area of vegetation, the fine features of the subak system, or the farmers tending to their fields. You will be in awe of the breathtaking backdrop that the terraces' symmetrical patterns produce.

The Tegallalang Rice Terraces are proof of the Balinese people's close ties to their homeland and their expertise in taking care of the environment. The physical splendor of Bali and its rich cultural legacy can both be appreciated by traveling to this magical location.

Nusa Penida - Undiscovered Beaches and Immaculate Waters

Southeast of Bali in Indonesia is the lovely island of Nusa Penida, which is renowned for its secret coves and turquoise waters. It's a well-liked place for tourists looking for tranquillity and natural beauty away from the busy throng.

You can visit the following secluded beaches and gorgeous locations in Nusa Penida:

One of the most well-known locations on Nusa Penida is without a doubt Kelingking Beach. Overlooking a spotless white sand beach and blue waters, it has a striking T-shaped-shaped cliff formation. The strenuous descent to the beach is well worth it because of the beautiful vistas.

Crystal Bay: As its name suggests, Crystal Bay is well-known for having seas that are crystal clear, which make it an excellent location for diving and snorkeling. Numerous marine species, such as vibrant corals and tropical fish, call the area home. The sandy beach is a great place to unwind, enjoy the sunshine, or go swimming in the serene waters.

Atuh Beach is a secret paradise tucked away in a quiet bay. You must down a long stairway built into the side of a cliff to get to this beach, but the effort is worth it for the stunning beach's fluffy white sand, crystal-clear seas, and soaring limestone cliffs. It's a great place to unwind and take in the breathtaking scenery.

Broken Beach (Pasih Uug) is a distinctive natural structure distinguished by a natural archway that extends across crystalline seas. It's an amazing sight to see the ocean water flowing into a pool that is encircled by cliffs. Swimming is not permitted at the beach, however there are great photo possibilities.

A natural infinity pool created by a rock formation is called Angel's Billabong, and it is close to Broken Beach. At low tide, a captivating natural pool is formed by the clear turquoise waters, luring guests to take a dip and take in the surroundings.

Peguyangan Beach and Waterfall: Peguyangan Waterfall is not like other waterfalls. To get to it, you must descend a flight of blue stairs that lead down a cliff and into the water. The beach is rocky and has clear waters at the bottom, making it a tranquil place to unwind and enjoy the wonders of nature.

When visiting these beaches, keep in mind to take the required safety precautions, such as dressing properly for the weather and drinking plenty of water. Additionally, it's critical to pay attention to the tides and currents, especially if you intend to swim or snorkel. Overall, for nature lovers and those looking for a peaceful getaway, Nusa Penida's undiscovered beaches offer a unique experience.

CHAPTER 4

EXPLORING BALINESE CUISINE

Balinese Cuisine Overview

The island's cultural legacy includes the distinctive and significant Balinese cuisine. Its cuisine is rooted in history, spirituality, and a profound love and respect for the natural world.

The foundation of food culture is fresh ingredients and traditional cooking techniques. Balinese food, which is distinguished by strong flavors, unique spices, and fresh ingredients, is a celebration of the island's gastronomic abundance and is served in the shadow of lava-filled volcanoes.

It is recommended for visitors to Bali to learn about the island's culinary legacy by visiting traditional markets, sampling regional cuisines, or enrolling in a cooking class.

Visitors can better appreciate the culture and customs of the island by enjoying traditional Balinese cuisine. Visitors should ensure that their time in Bali includes participating in the island's distinctive and significant gastronomic culture.

Popular Balinese Dishes and Ingredients

In a range of mouthwatering recipes, Bali is renowned for its strong flavors, unusual spices, and fresh ingredients. The following are some of Bali's most well-known dishes:

Suckling Pig On The Grill

A whole pig is stuffed with a combination of herbs, spices, and vegetables to make Babi Guling, a Balinese meal that is then roasted over an open flame.

The outcome is juicy, delicious meat that is crispy on the outside and within. Usually, sambal, a hot chili sauce, rice, and veggies are served with babi guling.

B. Nasi Campur, which is mixed rice with a variety of toppings

A common Balinese cuisine called Nasi Campur consists of a plate of rice topped with chicken or pig, veggies, tofu, and tempeh, among other ingredients. A boiled egg and sambal are frequently included with the dish.

C.Skewers of minced meat, Sate Lilit

Sate Lilit is a sort of Balinese skewer made with minced meat that has been combined with spices and coconut milk, usually chicken or fish. The meat are wrapped around a bamboo skewer. After that, the skewers are roasted over an open flame to give them a delectable smoky flavor.

D. (Spicy Salad) Lawar

Lawar is a typical Balinese salad that combines blanched vegetables (such as jackfruit, young papaya, and fern tips) with fresh grated coconut and minced meat (such as chicken, pork, or beef).

4.3 Recommended Restaurant and Warungs

1. Restaurants serving Italian food include Da Mario's Trattoria, La Pergola, and Il Gatto Nero in Rome and Cernobbio, respectively.

2. Mexican restaurants include El Fogón in Playa del Carmen, Mexico City 's Contramar, and Cabo San Lucas' La Cocina de Frida.

3. There are other restaurants serving Japanese food around the world, including Sukiyabashi Jiro in Tokyo, Matsuhisa in Beverly Hills, and Nobu.

4. Indian food with an accent, New Delhi, India

- Gaggan (Bangkok, Thailand) - Bukhara (New Delhi, India)

5. Le Bernardin (Paris, France), a French restaurant
L'Ambroisie and Pierre Gagnaire, both from Paris, France

6. Nahm (Bangkok, Thailand) serves Thai food
Issaya Siamese Club and Bo.Lan, both in Bangkok, Thailand

7. Din Tai Fung (Taipei, Taiwan), a Chinese restaurant
- Haidilao Hot Pot, with locations throughout the world.
Beijing, China's Quanjude

8. Restaurants serving Indonesian food include Warung Wardani in Ubud, Bali, Ikan Bakar Cianjur in Jakarta, Indonesia, and Warung Nasi Ayam Bu Oki in Surabaya, Indonesia.

El Celler de Can Roca (Girona, Spain) is a popular Spanish restaurant.
Barcelona, Spain's Tickets; San Sebastian, Spain's Arzak

10. American restaurants: Eleven Madison Park in New York City; Alinea in Chicago; Chez Panisse in Berkeley.

CHAPTER 5

OUTDOOR ADVENTURE

Surfing and other water sports

Surfers and water sports lovers from all over the world flock to Bali, Indonesia, because of its beautiful beaches. The island has a variety of surf breaks and a selection of water sports. In Bali, the following are some well-liked choices for water sports and surfing:

Bali has superb surfing conditions for both novice and seasoned surfers. The following are a few well-known surf locations:

Due to its calm waves, Kuta Beach, which is towards the southwest, is an ideal place for new surfers to learn the sport.

Uluwatu: This well-known surfing location on the Bukit Peninsula is noted for its top-notch waves and draws expert surfers. For people of varying ability levels, Uluwatu provides a variety of portions.

Known for its strong and difficult waves, Padang Padang is a well-known reef break close to Uluwatu and is a favorite among seasoned surfers.

Canggu: This region offers a range of breaks appropriate for travelers of all skill levels. Popular locations in Canggu include Berawa Beach and Echo Beach.

Kiteboarding: Due to Bali's regular wind conditions, kiteboarding is a popular activity there. Kite schools that rent out equipment and offer training may be found in Tanjung Benoa, Nusa Dua, and other well-liked kiteboarding locations.

Bali's tranquil waters are ideal for stand-up paddleboarding (SUP), which is a fun activity. Take SUP yoga lessons or hire

SUPs to explore the nearby beaches of Sanur, Seminyak, and Nusa Dua.

Water sports like jet skiing are very common in Bali. Many beaches, including Tanjung Benoa, have jet ski rentals and guided trips so you may experience the rush of slicing through the surf.

Scuba diving and snorkeling: Bali is well-known for its thriving marine life and gorgeous dive spots. In places like Tulamben, Amed, and Nusa Penida, you may go scuba diving and snorkeling and explore coral reefs, come in contact with manta rays, and even go to the well-known USAT Liberty shipwreck.

White Water Rafting: For an exhilarating adventure, try white water rafting on one of Bali's rivers, including the Ayung River close to Ubud. Rafting excursions through the lush forest are led by knowledgeable guides, providing an exhilarating and picturesque experience.

It's crucial to remember that safety comes first whenever you participate in water sports. Verify that the companies you hire are reliable, adhere to safety precautions, and are knowledgeable about regional factors like tides and currents.

Swimming and Snorkeling

Scuba diving and snorkeling enthusiasts frequently travel to Bali, Indonesia. The island has many diving spots with colorful coral reefs, a variety of marine life, and great visibility. Some important information regarding snorkeling and scuba diving in Bali is provided below:

Scuba diving

Dive Sites: Bali has a wide variety of dive sites that are suitable for divers of all abilities. Amed, Nusa Penida, Nusa Lembongan, Tulamben, and Padang Bai are a few of the well-known locations.

Marine Life: Bali's surrounding waters support a diverse marine ecosystem. Divers can come across a variety of marine life, such as vibrant coral formations, turtles, reef sharks, manta rays, and even the elusive mola mola (sunfish), depending on the time of year.

diving Centers: There are a large number of diving shops and operators in Bali that provide guided dives, equipment rentals, and beginner dive courses. It's crucial to select a trustworthy operator with knowledgeable instructors and up-to-date equipment.

Dive Courses: Bali is a great spot to learn scuba diving if you've never done it or if you want to improve your abilities. Numerous dive shops provide classes in everything from open water diver certifications for beginners to advanced specialties like wreck diving and underwater photography.

Snorkeling:

Spots for Snorkeling: Bali has some great places for snorkeling, especially along its eastern and southern coasts. Amed, Padang Bai, Blue Lagoon, Menjangan Island, and Nusa Lembongan are just a few of the well-known snorkeling locations.

Equipment: Dive shops and merchants at the beach sell snorkeling equipment for rent. A mask, snorkel, and fins are frequently included. In some locations, life jackets or flotation devices are also available for increased safety.

Marine Diversity: Just below the water's surface, snorkelers can observe colorful fish, magnificent coral gardens, and other marine life. Look out for colorful species including angelfish, parrotfish, and clownfish.

Safety: While snorkeling is generally seen to be safe, it's important to be aware of your surroundings, water currents, and keep coral reefs away from your contact. Consider taking a guided snorkeling tour for enhanced safety and local knowledge if you're new to snorkeling or are unfamiliar with the area.

General Tips

Finest Time to Visit: Bali's dry season, which runs from April to October, provides the finest diving and snorkeling opportunities because to its calmer waters and superior visibility.

The island of Bali has a tropical environment with pleasant temperatures all year long. It is usually comfortable to dive in a short wetsuit or rash guard when the water is between 26°C and 29°C (79°F and 84°F).

Environmental Awareness: Due to the fragility of Bali's marine ecosystems, it is essential to dive and snorkel responsibly. Use reef-safe sunscreen to reduce negative effects, refrain from touching or harming the coral, and don't feed the fish.

Health and Safety: Ascertain that you have adequate travel insurance that includes diving and snorkeling. If you intend to scuba dive, you can think about obtaining a dive medical certificate in advance to make sure you are in good health.

To ensure a fun and rewarding underwater experience, arrange your diving and snorkeling excursions in Bali with trustworthy operators, abide by safety precautions, and respect the marine ecosystem.

White-Water Rafting

White water rafting is a well-liked adventure sport in Bali that gives you the chance to explore the island's lovely rivers and breathtaking natural settings. Please be aware that although I can give you general information about white water rafting, specifics like the operators, costs, and availability may change over time. If you want the most recent information, it's always best to check with nearby tour companies or run an online search.

The Ayung River and the Telaga Waja River are the two most well-liked options among the white water rafting rivers in Bali. Here is a summary of these rafting locations:

Ayung River: Situated in Ubud, the Ayung River offers an exhilarating rafting experience together with rich vegetation and beautiful scenery. A safety orientation and equipment distribution usually kick off a rafting tour. After that, you'll go out on a thrilling excursion through class II and III rapids while taking in the sights of the nearby tropical forests, waterfalls, and stone carvings. Both inexperienced and seasoned rafters can safely use the Ayung River.

Telaga Waja River: Located in the east of Bali, the Telaga Waja River is well-known for its more difficult rapids, making it the perfect place for anyone looking for an exhilarating adventure. The river's spectacular vistas of the surrounding rice terraces and lush woodlands are provided by its deep valleys. When rafting on the Telaga Waja River, class III and IV rapids are typically encountered, making for an exciting experience for rafters with some prior experience.

It is advised to reserve a tour with a reliable rafting operator in order to partake in white water rafting. Transport to and from your hotel, knowledgeable guides, safety gear (including helmets and life jackets), and a buffet-style dinner are typically included in these tours. Although the rafting trip's length can vary, it usually lasts a few hours.

White water rafting has inherent risks, therefore you must always put safety first, pay attention to your guides' instructions, and prioritize safety at all times. Prior to participating in any outdoor activity, put on proper attire, such as a swimsuit or quick-drying shorts, water shoes or strapped sandals.

Last but not least, keep in mind that the availability of white water rafting tours might be impacted by the weather and river conditions. If you want to go rafting while visiting Bali, it's a good idea to check the weather forecast and get in touch with regional tour operators in advance.

Have fun on your Bali whitewater rafting excursion!

TREKKING AND HIKING

There are many fantastic options for hikers and trekkers on Bali, an Indonesian island renowned for its breathtaking landscapes and rich cultural legacy. Bali's stunning natural scenery offers an enthralling backdrop for outdoor excursions, including lush rice terraces, volcanic peaks, secret waterfalls, and old temples. Here are a few of Bali's well-liked places for hiking and trekking:

Mount Batur is an active volcano in the Kintamani area that makes for an enjoyable trekking excursion. Early in the morning, the climb to the summit starts so that you may see the magnificent sunrise. The trail is generally mild, suited for most fitness levels, and the ascent typically takes two hours.

Mount Agung: A sacred mountain and Bali's highest peak, Mount Agung presents a strenuous trekking experience. It normally takes five to seven hours to reach the summit and demands a high level of physical fitness. The peak offers expansive views of the island as compensation.

Campuhan Ridge Walk: The Campuhan Ridge Walk, located in Ubud, is a leisurely and picturesque hike through verdant foliage, rice fields, and tiny towns. For those seeking a more leisurely hike with stunning scenery and photo ops, it's a fantastic choice.

Sekumpul Waterfall: This undiscovered beauty can be found in Bali's northern region. You must descend steep slopes, cross streams, and make your way through dense woodland on the journey to the waterfall. You will be rewarded with the sight of numerous flowing waterfalls surrounded by breathtaking natural landscape, so the effort is worthwhile.

Gitgit Waterfall: Gitgit Waterfall in North Bali is another beautiful waterfall that is interesting to explore. Gitgit Waterfall is an accessible hike that can be paired with trips to adjacent rice terraces and traditional settlements.

Visit the West Bali National Park for a distinctive hiking experience. It has a variety of ecosystems, including mangroves, savannahs, and deep woods. Explore several routes, look for species like monkeys and deer, and take in the peace and quiet of nature.

In the Tabanan regency, Mount Batukaru is a less-traveled hiking trail that is ideal for people wanting a tranquil and pleasant hike. You can see uncommon bird species along the walk, which passes through ancient temples and thick rainforests.

It's important to think about your physical condition, the weather, and safety precautions before starting a climbing or trekking excursion in Bali. To ensure a seamless and enjoyable experience, it is advised to travel with an experienced guide or join scheduled tours. Always drink enough of water, dress appropriately, and show respect for the surrounding environment and cultural practices.

Cycling and Mountain Biking

Cycling and mountain bike fans can find enough to do on Bali, a well-known Indonesian island noted for its breathtaking beaches and vibrant culture. Bali is a terrific location for both relaxing rides and tough off-road experiences thanks to its varied topography, beautiful scenery, and cultural attractions. Here is some information to assist you in organizing your mountain bike and cycling excursions in Bali:

Ubud: Ubud is a well-liked cycling destination in Bali because it provides picturesque routes through rice fields, ancient towns, and beautiful forests. For an excursion through the picturesque countryside surrounding Ubud, you can rent a bicycle or sign up for a guided cycling trip.

Mount Batur: For lovers of mountain riding, Mount Batur is a destination that cannot be missed. In the northeastern region of Bali, Mount Batur has exhilarating downhill courses for skiers of all abilities. The trails offer breathtaking panoramas of the surroundings as they wind their way down through volcanic terrain.

Rice Terraces in Jatiluwih: Jatiluwih is a UNESCO World Heritage Site famous for its stunning rice terraces. This region offers a fantastic opportunity for leisurely cycling, allowing you to take in the magnificent scenery while bicycling through the thick vegetation.

Visit West Bali National Park if you're searching for a more challenging mountain biking experience. There are several different ecosystems in the park, including coastal regions, savannahs, and rainforests. While taking in the picturesque beauty of the park, you can explore off-road routes and come across unusual creatures.

East Bali: The island of Bali's eastern region is home to a variety of cycling routes, including highways that go along the coast and through old-fashioned towns. You may travel to places like Candidasa and Amed, where you can travel along stunning coastline roads and stop at historical sites along the way.

Numerous tour companies in Bali provide guided bicycle trips that are catered to various preferences and skill levels. These trips frequently include the rental of bicycles, transportation, and knowledgeable guides who can show you the best cycling routes while sharing insights into the local way of life and tourist spots.

When mountain biking or cycling in Bali, put safety first. Always use a helmet, observe all traffic laws, and pay attention to the state of the roads. Maintaining proper hydration is also crucial, particularly given Bali's tropical temperature.

CHAPTER 6

BALINESE FESTIVALS AND TRADITIONS

Balinese Hinduism and religious customs, paragraph

The truly fantastic culture and religion that you may observe being practiced all across Bali is one of the island's distinctive draws.

Hinduism in Balinese culture is very unique; it is characterized by year-round festivities, ceremonies, and customs.

Hindus in Bali celebrate everything, including weddings, births, new cars, books in the classroom, and full moons.

Here is more information on Balinese Hinduism, a really rich and fascinating religion. Here are some significant features of Balinese Hinduism and its practices:

1. Beliefs and Deities: Hinduism in Bali worships a pantheon of deities, with the Trimurti (Brahma, Vishnu, and Shiva) regarded as the paramount deities. Dewi Sri, the goddess of rice and fertility, Saraswati, the goddess of learning and the arts, and Ganesh, the remover of obstacles, are a few additional significant deities. The ghosts of departed ancestors are respected and play a significant role in daily life.

2. Tri Hita Karana is a central idea in Balinese Hinduism that places emphasis on the harmonious coexistence of humans, nature, and divinity. It demonstrates that harmony and balance are necessary for health and wealth.

3. Temple Worship: Puras, or temples, are important in Balinese Hinduism. Bali has a huge number of temples, from modest village shrines to expansive complexes. There are normally three temples in each village: a Pura Puseh (temple of origin), a

Pura Desa (village temple), and a Pura Dalem (temple for the dead). Hindus in Bali frequent temples frequently for prayers, rituals, and festivals.

4. Offerings and rites: Canang sari, or offerings, are an essential component of Balinese Hindu rites. The flowers, grains, and other symbolic goods are enclosed in these offerings, which are created from woven palm leaves. They are erected in revered locations such as household shrines, temples, and other buildings to pay homage to the gods and ancestors.

5. Holidays & Religious festivities: Bali is well known for its colorful religious holidays and festivities. The most important holiday is Nyepi, which is also known as the Balinese New Year and is a day of reflection. Other significant festivals are Galungan, Kuningan, Saraswati, and Odalan, which are commemorated via elaborate rituals, processions, dances, and music.

6. Balinese Ritual Dances: Hindu rites and celebrations in Bali include dance as an essential component. There are several traditional dances, including the Barong, Legong, and Kecak dances, which frequently represent mythological tales and act as a means of spiritual expression.

7. Caste System: The Hinduism of Bali still uses a modified version of the caste system that originated in India. Comparatively speaking, the Indian caste system is more rigid and hierarchical than the one in Bali. It mostly affects social commitments and relationships within the society.

Hinduism in Bali is a distinctive religion that has been practiced continuously for many years. Due to its unique rituals, beliefs, and modes of devotion, it differs from other forms of Hinduism.

This really unusual religion is highly worth knowing about because of its heavy emphasis on god, goddesses, ancestors, and spirits.

BALINESE FESTIVALS AND CELEBRATIONS

With its gorgeous beaches, mountains, and volcanoes, Bali is an exceptionally beautiful and culturally diverse place. Bali is unique because of its charming festivals and celebrations, among other things. These occasions serve as a showcase for the local traditions and customs and are joyfully observed all year long. Each Bali spirit festival is full with joyful celebration, whether it be the musical performances at Kuningan or the complex parades of Galungan. There is always something special to uncover when exploring Bali's celebrations, from Nyepi's day of quiet to Odalan's vibrant dance performances.

You can witness the splendor and customs of Bali's culture firsthand if you visit the island during these festivals. It's crucial to be aware that ceremonies may cause road closures, and that during major festivals, businesses will also be closed. Tourists are urged to show patience, respect, and appreciation as these events and festivals are sacred to the Balinese and a part of what makes their culture so lovely and open to foreigners.

Let's examine what makes Balinese festivals so spectacular as we dig into the enthralling realm of Bali.

Galungan and Kuningan.

The Balinese calendar has two of Bali's most revered festivals, Galungan and Kuningan, which happen every 210 days. They animate the island with their vivid hues, upbeat music, and ornate decorations, most notably the penjor, bamboo poles with offerings dangling at the ends, which line the streets. Galungan, which heralds the victory of good over evil, marks the start of the festival. After ten days, there is Kuningan, a time to praise nature for her abundance and ask God and your ancestors for favors.

A. Melasti

Three days prior to Nyepi, the Balinese New Year, is the traditional Hindu festival of Melasti in Bali. Balinese Hindus congregate on beaches while dressed in traditional white attire to cleanse their souls by taking sea baths, reciting sacred mantras, and praying to Shiva for spiritual enlightenment and abundance in the next year. Through the performance of traditional dances, the sharing of regional cuisine, and the presenting of offerings at religious shrines, the event also fosters community and family unity. Locals can reaffirm their beliefs, celebrate new beginnings, and reconnect with their cultural heritage at Melasti.

- Nyepi

Nyepi is the most significant, revered, and holy day of the year. Every year, it happens the day following the new moon in March. According to the Saka calendar, a new year is ushered in during this Hindu festival. Additionally, it represents a time of introspection for all Bali people. It's called "The Day of Silence," and it's totally forbidden to travel, work, or use energy. It's even against the law for tourists to leave their hotels!

But this isn't merely a peaceful holiday; its fundamental principles are spiritual convictions. In Hindu mythology, Nyepi commemorated the triumph of good over evil when demons who sought to disturb holy rituals overcame the gods. Ogoh-ogoh statues of monsters or gods are created as part of the celebrations leading up to the day and paraded around the village streets before being torched that evening. Large bonfires are also lit in numerous communities throughout Bali.

- The Festival of Omed-Omedan

Every year in Banjar Kaja Sesetan, Denpasar, Bali, the Omed-Omedan Festival is a thrilling and distinctive occasion. It is observed the day following Nyepi and is also referred to as "The Kissing Ritual" because hundreds of single men and women between the ages of 17 and 30 get together to share a day of joy and camaraderie. Couples are brought together to hug and then kiss while bystanders throw water on them as a purifying symbol after the men and women split. Locals and visitors come together for the event in a joyful celebration of life and the purging of the past. It is simple to understand why the Omed-Omedan Festival is one of Bali's most well-liked occasions given its great vigor and infectious vibrancy.

The Saraswati

In Bali, there is a unique festival called Saraswati that honors the Hindu goddess of wisdom and understanding. At shrines all around Bali, offerings are made during this time. To pray for success in their education, businesses, and other endeavors, people go to temples. Saraswati festivals play a significant role in Bali culture because they encourage coexistence between humans and environment, foster information sharing, and deepen bonds between neighbors by fostering respect for one another's cultures.

Tumpek Landep.

Every 210 days, Bali celebrates Tumpek Landep, a festival honoring weapons and particularly metals. Hindus think that these objects have spiritual qualities that can shield users from danger. Hindus from Bali offer prayers in temples all throughout the island while using various offerings, including flowers, food, and incense. To honor the gods that protect their homes, they frequently erect traditional Balinese daggers outside of them. Tumpek Landep serves as a reminder of the value of defending against threats while maintaining domestic tranquility.

Hindus on the island pay great regard to the metal religious objects on this day of Tumpek Landep, especially the Keris, which is now considered to have spiritual force and is a part of the physical cultural heritage.

- Odal

On the anniversary of the dedication of Bali's Hindu temples, Odalan is observed. The Odalan festival, which is based on the Balinese calendar, has a different date for each temple in Bali. Normally, the holiday is observed every 210 days. Balinese Hindus attend their neighborhood temples during the Odalan festival dressed in traditional attire and bring offerings of food, flowers, and incense to honor the gods. Throughout the event, a number of ceremonies, dances, and rituals are performed. Hindus in Bali use the holiday as a significant opportunity to recommit to their faith and to enhance their sense of community.

- The Festival of Perang Pandan

Tenganan Village hosts the Perang Pandan Festival, commonly referred to as Mekare-kare, which is a yearly celebration. Men from the hamlet engage in a traditional battle using prickly pandan leaves as weapons. Every year, on the day following the Galungan celebration, the festival is held, typically in May or June. It is a distinctive and vibrant festival that draws tourists from all around the world.

In a fake combat that takes place during the event, men from the hamlet use strips of pandan leaf that have been knotted into a little bundle. The two men then engage in combat, seeking to avoid being struck while attacking their adversaries with the prickly leaves. The combat goes on until one fighter concedes or is pronounced the victor. The celebration is thought to be a method to honor Indra, the Hindu god of rain and war.

- Buffalo Races in Makepung

A customary cultural celebration known as the Makepung Buffalo Races takes place in Bali's Jembrana region. Farmers compete in this unusual and thrilling race on the backs of two water buffalo that have been carefully trained and adorned for the event. Every year from July through November, the Makepung races are staged, typically on weekends. Large numbers of spectators go to the event to support their favorite teams and take part in the joyous atmosphere. The races serve as both a traditional contest and a method to celebrate farming culture and forge stronger ties among farmers.

Farmers compete against one another with their adorned buffaloes along a 150- to 200-meter course. Farmers use customary bamboo poles to control the buffaloes, which are capable of traveling at speeds of up to 60 km/h. Based on the buffaloes' speed, style, and decorations, the races are evaluated.

BALI ARTS FESTIVAL

Since 1982, the Bali Arts Festival has been hosted annually in Denpasar's Art Centre, highlighting the skills of local artists in Balinese art and culture, including woodcarving, Balinese painting, metalwork, batik weaving, and traditional song and dance performances. Local cuisine, kid-friendly interactive activities, and cross-cultural interactions between communities in Indonesia and elsewhere are available to visitors. The festival is one of the most well-known occasions in Indonesia since it fosters intercultural communication, knowledge exchange, literary arts, and love and relationships. The Bali Arts Festival is a must-attend event for everyone, whether you enjoy art or are searching for enjoyable things to do with your loved ones.

- Ubud Writers and Readers Festival

Every year in Ubud, there is a festival honoring writers, artists, and ideas from all over the world called the Ubud Writers and Readers Festival. Since its inception in 2004, the festival has developed into one of Southeast Asia's most prestigious literary gatherings, drawing a broad and global audience of authors, readers, and thinkers. The festival offers a wide range of activities, including performances, literary workshops, panel discussions, book launches, and opportunities for attendees to interact with writers and other fans. The Ubud Writers and Readers Festival fosters a sense of community among those who share a passion for literature and the arts by placing a strong emphasis on cultural exchange and debate.

Bali Events & Festivals Calendar
The dates fluctuate yearly since many festivities in Bali follow the 210-day Balinese calendar and lunar cycles. The dates for each year can be found online, or

you can ask our staff at Bali Res Centre for further details.

For those interested in learning about its intriguing festivals and celebrations, Bali is a delight. There are numerous opportunities to immerse oneself in this distinctive culture, from the lively Galungan and Kuningan to the meditative Nyepi. The festivals and celebrations of Bali draw tourists from all over the world. Year after year, visitors, culture buffs, and environment enthusiasts are awestruck and delighted by this island.

Traditional Arts and Crafts

The "Island of the Gods," Bali, has a vibrant cultural history, and traditional arts and crafts are very important to the island's identity. Painting, woodcarving, silverwork, textiles, and traditional dance are just a few of the many artistic mediums used in Balinese art. Here are a few examples of Bali's traditional arts and crafts:

Painting: The elaborate details, vivid colors, and extensive symbolism of Balinese paintings set them apart from other styles. Traditional painting techniques include Kamasan, which illustrates Hindu myths, and Ubud, which represents ordinary Balinese life. These paintings are frequently produced on a variety of surfaces, including canvas, wood, and paper.

Balinese woodcarving is recognized around the world for its elaborate designs and superb craftsmanship. Wood is intricately carved by skilled artists into furniture, masks, sculptures, and decorative things. Woodcarvings frequently draw their inspiration from Balinese mythology, Hindu epics, or organic patterns.

Silverwork: The gold and silver artistry produced in the village of Celuk is renowned. Beautiful jewelry, including earrings, necklaces, rings, and bracelets, are made by Balinese artists utilizing age-old techniques. Balinese silverwork frequently includes elaborate motifs, granulation, and filigree work.

Textiles: Bali is well known for its hand-woven batik and ikat textiles. While ikat entails tying and dying threads prior to weaving, batik is a traditional technique that uses wax and dye to create beautiful patterns on cloth. Clothing, scarves, tablecloths, and other decorative things are all made from these materials.

Basketry: Another ancient Balinese craft, basketry involves weaving natural materials like bamboo, rattan, and pandanus leaves. Using a variety of weaving techniques, artisans craft intricate baskets, trays, purses, and caps. These goods have both functional and aesthetic uses.

Dance and Music: The Barong dance and Legong dance are two highly regarded Balinese traditional dance genres. These dances feature traditional Gamelan music and frequently reflect mythological tales. Bronze percussion instruments are played in complicated patterns by gamelan ensembles to create a fascinating sound.

Stone Carving: Bali is renowned for its heritage in stone carving. With the help of volcanic stone, such as limestone and sandstone, artists create detailed statues, reliefs, and decorative pieces. Temples, palaces, and other cultural places all throughout the island include these stone carvings.

Shadow puppetry, also known as Wayang Kulit, is a traditional storytelling technique used in Bali. A puppeteer tells ancient and epic tales while intricately crafted leather puppets are moved behind a backlit screen.

These are only a few illustrations of Bali's traditional arts and crafts. The island's vibrant artistic traditions and cultural diversity continue to draw tourists from all over the world who value the beauty and workmanship of Balinese art.

PHOTOGRAPHY TIPS FOR YOUR SMARTPHONE OR DIGITAL CAMERA

KNOW YOUR CAMERA: Learn all there is to know about the settings, functions, and capabilities of your smartphone or digital camera. To understand what it is capable of, read the handbook and experiment with the various settings.

Keep the lens clean and free of dust and smudges to ensure sharp and clear photographs. For the best results, clean your lenses with a microfiber cloth or lens cleaner.

STRUCTURE IS IMPORTANT: To make visually appealing and balanced images, pay attention to composition by using the rule of thirds, leading lines, and framing.
Lighting is essential. Great photographs require excellent lighting. When the sun is just rising or setting, this is known as the

"golden hour," and it is the best time to take pictures.

STABILITY FOR SHARPNESS: To prevent camera shake, especially in low-light conditions or while utilizing slow shutter speeds, use a tripod or locate a firm surface.

To have more control over the exposure and create certain artistic effects, use manual exposure controls, such as aperture, shutter speed, and ISO, if at all practical.

FOCUS AND DEPTH OF FIELD: Be mindful of your focus points and depth of field. To make the background of a portrait blurry, use a shallow depth of field (big aperture), or for landscape photography, use a deep depth of field (small aperture).

A wider variety of light and shadow features can be captured by using the HDR or RAW modes, if they are offered. Use the RAW format for additional post-processing latitude.

Get closer to your subject or think about trimming in post-processing to maintain image quality instead of utilizing digital zoom.

EDIT AND IMPROVE: Use photo editing software or apps to post-process your images. To bring out the best in your photographs, adjust the exposure, contrast, colors, and sharpness.

Don't forget that practice makes perfect. To develop your photographic abilities, do new things and always take notes. Have fun shooting!

CHAPTER 7

PRACTICAL INFORMATION

Tips for Health and Safety

Priority one is safety. It's simple to forget that travelers are frequently the victims of minor crimes and ordinary scams with all the joy and excitement that traveling and visiting new places provide (not just in Bali, but in tourist hubs around the world).

This list of things you can do to keep yourself and your stuff safe in Bali has been put together because we want you all to love and appreciate Bali as much as we do and leave with only good memories.

Use only authorized money changers

2. Only ride a motorcycle if you are fully licensed and experienced.

3. Employ Trusted Transportation
4. When riding a bike or walking down the street, put your bags and phone away.
5. Avoid drinking or using tap water to brush your teeth.
6. Apply insect repellent
7.Use secure ATMs.
8.Utilize a VPN.
9. Obtain travel protection
10. Avoid Typical Scams

CURRENCY EXCHANGE AND MONEY

The currency of Indonesia is the Indonesian Rupiah. Rupiahs have the IDR currency code and the Rp currency sign.

If you wait until after you arrive in Bali to exchange your money, you will almost always get a higher rate. If you are concerned about landing in Bali without any money, you may always exchange a small sum of cash before you depart (in Australia, we advise doing this at Australia Post because there are no fees involved).

It's crucial to always exchange money at secure, well-known places while visiting Bali. Do not fall in to the temptation of street money changers offering an extremely high exchange rate,These street vendors are like magicians; they can make your money vanish right before your eyes!

When converting money into rupiah, there are a lot of zeros, and these shady money changers will profit from that. Even if you manage to outwit them, you won't ever receive the high rate they are promising; instead, you will only receive your original currency back.

ACCESS TO THE INTERNET AND COMMUNICATION

Today, Bali has a respectable communications infrastructure. Public phones, internet cafes, and decent GSM service may be found practically everywhere there is a street.

Mobile devices

Mobile phone coverage is great in the most of the main tourist areas, however service is scarce in Bali's more isolated regions. We urge anyone visiting Bali with a mobile phone to confirm their network's policy on international roaming before departing.

GSM is the cellular standard in Indonesia. You have the choice to buy a prepaid calling card to make outgoing calls at a lower cost than calling on your home SIM if you do decide to bring your mobile phone to Bali. They can be purchased from a number of stores with the logos of the service providers, including IM3, Telkomsel, Satelindo, and Pro XL.

Internet access

There are many internet cafés in Bali where you can check your mail. All of the major tourist destinations, including Kuta, Nusa Dua, Sanur, Legian, Denpasar, Ubud, Candidasa, and Lovina, have Internet cafes. The majority of large hotels will have an on-site business center or internet cafe.

You should ask your ISP about roaming arrangements if you plan to carry your laptop. You can also connect to Telkomnet, which does not require registration.

Magazines And Newspapers

Numerous street vendors are willing to offer you their two-day-old Australian and international newspapers. Never forget to haggle! The Jakarta Post, Herald Tribune, and Asian Wall Street Journal are just a few of the daily local English-language publications that are available.

Numerous free travel publications are routinely distributed at hotels and shopping malls. Get your issue today for the most recent news and information.

Mailing Services

Although stamps bought outside of post offices may cost more than twice as much as face value, postcards and letters can be sent from hotels and shops. There are rumors that postcards and letters mailed from hotels and shops never reach their intended recipient. Find the closest post office, buy your stamps there, then send your postcards and/or letters from there.

Every large town and hamlet has a post office, which is open Monday through Thursday from 8 a.m. to 2 p.m., Friday from 8 a.m. to noon, and Saturday from 8 a.m. to 1 p.m. The central post office is open everyday from 7.30 am to 8.30 pm and on Sundays from 8 am to 8 pm. It is situated in Denpasar on Jl. Raya Puputan, Renon.

USEFUL PHRASES AND LOCAL ETIQUETTE

Useful Phrases:

Hello - Halo
Thank you - Terima kasih
Yes - Ya
No - Tidak
Excuse me - Permisi
Sorry - Maaf
How are you? - Apa kabar?
Goodbye - Selamat tinggal
Can you help me? - Bisa bantu saya?
Where is the restroom? - Di mana kamar mandi?

Local Etiquette:

A friendly greeting is appreciated by Balinese people. It is courteous to welcome somebody when you meet them with the Balinese phrase "Om Swastiastu," which means "May peace be with you" (pronounced "ohm suh-was-tee-as-too").

Bali is renowned for its stunning beaches and laid-back vibe, but when visiting temples or more traditional places, it's necessary to dress modestly. Both men and women's shoulders and knees should be covered.

Temples: It's crucial to respect temples because they are sacred sites in Bali. Remember to take off your shoes before entering a temple, and don the sarong and sash that are offered there if you are not dressed appropriately.

Respect and decorum are things that Balinese people place a high value on. When speaking to locals, be sure to use polite expressions and gestures like "thank you" and "please." Even if there are challenges or arguments, always remember to talk in a polite and calm manner.

The right hand, or both hands, should be used when offering or receiving anything. The left hand is seen as filthy and is not to be used in polite society.

Public Displays of Affection: Bali is a well-known tourist destination, but public displays of affection, particularly in more traditional places, are typically frowned upon. Keeping demonstrations of affection secret and exercising restraint is advised.

Shoes: It's polite to take your shoes off while entering homes, temples, or even some stores. It will be clear if you should take off your shoes based on the footwear of those around you, so pay attention to their shoes.
Names used by Balinese people: Family names are not typically used and most

Balinese individuals have just one name. Addressing someone with Mr. or Mrs it is customary. followed by their first name because using their complete name may lead to misunderstandings. With a variety of cultural practices and customs, Bali is a diverse place. When traveling to any other nation, it's a good idea to respect and adhere to the local traditions and customs.

CHAPTER 8

BEYOND BALI

Bali Day Tours,

Beautiful beaches, a lively culture, and beautiful scenery are all hallmarks of Bali, Indonesia. There are a number of excellent day trip choices if you want to venture outside the island's boundaries. Some well-liked day tours from Bali are listed below:

Nusa Penida: This stunning island, which is southeast of Bali, is well-known for its towering cliffs, unspoiled shorelines, and blue waters. Kelingking Beach, Angel's Billabong, and Broken Beach are just a few of the sites you can visit. Snorkeling, diving, and soaking in the gorgeous scenery are all excellent here.

Ubud: Located just one hour's drive from Bali's busiest tourist attractions, Ubud offers a peaceful respite from the city's noise and activity. The town of Ubud, which is considered to be the cultural center of Bali, is well-known for its verdant rice terraces, traditional markets, art galleries, and historic temples like the Goa Gajah (Elephant Cave) and the Ubud Monkey Forest.

Mount Batur: If you like to take on new challenges, think about hiking up Mount Batur in the morning. Bali's active volcano, which is situated in the island's middle highlands, provides sweeping vistas of the whole thing. You can witness a breathtaking sunrise from the summit after the trek, which often begins in the early morning hours.

Gili Islands: The Gili Islands are worth noting because they are close to Bali, even though they are not really day trips. The three beautiful islands of Gili Trawangan, Gili Meno, and Gili Air are renowned for their clear waters, white sand beaches, and laid-back atmosphere. Take a swift boat from Bali to one of these idyllic tropical islands, where you may spend a night or two exploring.

Tegalalang Rice Terraces: The Tegalalang Rice Terraces are a well-liked spot for photographers and others who enjoy the outdoors and are located close to Ubud. Terraced rice fields provide beautiful scenery and a look at traditional Balinese agriculture. To have a closer look at this breathtaking natural beauty, you can stroll around the region or rent a bicycle.

Tanah Lot Temple: Situated on a rocky outcrop along Bali's western coast, Tanah Lot Temple is one of Bali's most iconic landmarks. Offering breathtaking views of the sun setting, the temple is located above the water. You may learn a lot about

Balinese spirituality and culture at this well-known pilgrimage site.

You may take day trips from Bali to places like these, to name a few. This stunning island has much to offer everyone, whether they are looking for culture, relaxation, or adventure. To get the most out of your day travels, remember to schedule your trips in advance and think about your transit alternatives.

Taking a Tour to other Indonesian Islands

Many of Indonesia's top tourist destinations, it's hard to believe, are still mostly undiscovered by visitors. Over 17,000 stunning islands make up Indonesia, the majority of which have not yet been seen.

Bali is a great island to visit for a holiday (don't get me wrong, it is), but for years it has been plagued by overdevelopment and overtourism.

In addition to other things, visiting other Indonesian islands will allow you to witness smoldering volcanoes, sulfur lakes, pink sand beaches, lush jungles, unusual fauna, and much more.

Being that Indonesia is my second home (and my wife's actual home!), we've had the opportunity to travel extensively there and have even visited some of the most remote Indonesian islands.

Here is a comprehensive list of all the top tourist destinations in Indonesia, except Bali. If you've visited an Indonesian island that isn't included here, please let us know.

1. Komodo Island: This island, which is a part of the Komodo National Park, is well-known for housing Komodo dragons, the largest reptiles in the world. The island also has wonderful diving chances, clean beaches, and breathtaking scenery.

2. Raja Ampat Islands: These West Papuan islands are renowned for their extraordinary marine biodiversity. The region is home to beautiful coral reefs, pristine waters, and a wide variety of marine life, making it a snorkelers' and divers' paradise.

3. Borneo (Kalimantan): Borneo, the third-largest island in the globe, is shared by Brunei, Indonesia, and Malaysia. The region of Indonesia known as Kalimantan is home to beautiful rainforests, orangutan reserves, and Dayak tribes that still practice their traditional ways.

4. Gili Islands: The Gili Islands, which are off the northwest coast of Lombok, are made up of three tiny islands: Gili Trawangan, Gili Air, and Gili Meno. These islands are well-known for their gorgeous beaches, clear waters, and laid-back vibe.

5. Flores Island: Located in eastern Indonesia, Flores is a beautiful island with a distinctive cultural history. Three vibrant

volcanic lakes may be found in the Kelimutu National Park, one of its highlights. Visit traditional communities to see the renowned Caci whip-fighting dance.

Sixth-largest island Sumatra has a variety of natural features to offer. It is the location of the UNESCO-listed Gunung Leuser National Park, where orangutans and other wildlife can be seen. Beautiful lakes, active volcanoes, and intriguing native cultures can all be found on Sumatra.

7. Sulawesi: This island, which resembles an orchid or a starfish, is renowned for both its unique culture and its natural splendors. Discover the elaborate ancient buildings and unusual funeral rites in the Toraja highlands. Don't miss Bunaken Marine Park, one of the best diving locations on earth.

8.Bali Island

Obviously, Asia's preferred vacation island! Bali must be mentioned before any other locations in Indonesia. Both luxury and budget travelers will find it to be heaven..

Bali offers easy access to waterfalls, jungles, cliffs, volcanoes, and other adventure-worthy locations. Or, if you prefer a more relaxed pace, Bali offers you beaches, temples, and rice terraces in addition to an infinite supply of top-notch dining establishments and massage parlors.

9.Nusa Penida Island
Nusa Penida, a beautiful island in Indonesia, is just 25 kilometers from Bali and is included in the Bali province.

Despite being significantly smaller than Bali, it features some of Indonesia's most unusual and breathtaking scenery. Despite the fact that we've been to Penida quite a few times over the years, it never gets boring.This island can be visited and returned from in a single day from Bali, but I believe it's best to stay for at least a few days to really explore it.

Some well-known natural attractions may be found there, such as the aptly called Diamond Beach and the dinosaur-shaped Kelingking Cliff.

Nusa Lembongan Island, number ten
Nusa Lembongan and Nusa Ceningan are two more nearby smaller islands that are part of the province of Bali in addition to the island of Nusa Penida.

The Devil's Tears, a charming tiny cliff location where you can watch the waves crash on the rocks, and Dream Beach, a white sand beach, are popular attractions on Nusa Lembongan.

From Bali, it's simple to reach Nusa Lembongan, and a quick and inexpensive boat journey will carry you from island to island within the Nusa group. Some visitors who are traveling Penida island even base themselves at Nusa Lembongan or Ceningan.

CHAPTER 9

TRAVEL RESOURCES AND ADVICE

9.1 Tips on packing and essential

Getting ready for your significant journey? For suggestions on what to carry to Indonesia's most visited island, Bali, consult our sample packing list.

For your journey to Bali, not much will be required. Bali is far from being a desert island, so if you forget something, you'll probably be able to find it locally anyhow! Instead, pack like an expert and carry less things. Consider taking advantage of the island's distinctive retail opportunities. More reason to visit the various boutique stores for beachwear and other goods that look well at home as well.

You won't just save space by not overpacking; you'll also have a chance to boast a little back home when folks inquire where you acquired that adorable sundress.

1. Bali Packing List: Clothing
Locals dress relatively conservatively, despite the stereotype that traveling on an exotic island means donning skimpy beachwear.

When you leave the beach, consider covering up. When visiting Hindu temples, revered locations like the Elephant Cave, or when touring small settlements in the island's interior, you should cover your shoulders and knees. Except while dining or clubbing at expensive establishments, casual clothing is acceptable for daily wear.

You won't have to worry about being cold on Bali unless you're using some of the public transit, which has powerful air conditioning. Choose cotton clothing that is lightweight because jeans are typically excessively hot and heavy. Clothes that dry quickly will also help, but avoid leaving costly athletic brands lying around to be stolen.

You won't need as much clothing as you might think; keep your Bali packing light and consider shopping locally if you run out of outfits to wear. Having said that, after perspiring all day, you'll likely want to switch tops every evening. You can locate several businesses that offer cheap laundry services if you're traveling for a long time. The price is normally determined by weight.

Pack everything you'll need to take advantage of the several yoga opportunities that will be available.

2. The Best Shoes for Bali

The standard footwear for Bali is only a pair of dependable flip-flops, as it is for the majority of Southeast Asia.

The entrance to some stores, temples, bars, and restaurants may require you to take off your shoes. Sandals with straps are more difficult to put on and take off rapidly than flip-flops. Keep a plastic bag nearby so you may carry your expensive sandals inside with you if you're concerned about leaving them at the door (they do occasionally disappear). All around the island, there are stores and kiosks where you may buy inexpensive flip-flops if you need them.

If you plan to climb Mount Batur or Gunung Agung, you'll need good hiking shoes or sandals. Sandals and flip-flops may be forbidden by certain nightclubs in Kuta and Seminyak. Bring decent shoes with you if you intend to go partying in any depth.

3. First Aid Supplies You Should Include

Your time on the island is valuable, and you don't want any irritating illness to interfere with it. You do not, however, need to carry any more medical equipment than a Green Beret medic. Fortunately, you don't need to initially visit a clinic because walk-in pharmacies provide almost everything you might possibly need, including prescription medications.

Just bring a compact, basic first aid kit for travel, and if more is needed, get it. I'm hoping that after a few too many beach cocktails, all you'll need is a couple of ibuprofen.

Tip: Anti-diarrhea medication like loperamide (Imodium) should be included in every first aid kit, but you shouldn't use it until using a restroom is not an option (such as if you'll be traveling for the entire day).

By preventing bothersome germs from naturally passing, antimotility medications may aggravate mild episodes of traveler's diarrhea.

4. Money and documents for Bali

Make duplicates of your passport, travel insurance policies, traveler's checks, and other essential travel documents that you should always have with you when you travel. To prevent a catastrophe if one or both copies are lost, diversify your copies by concealing them in both your day bag, money belt, and large luggage. Continually keep your passport and vaccination records on hand.

Send a mail if you want to contact banks with your credit card details (jumble the numbers so that only you can decipher them) and emergency phone numbers. If you intend to apply for tourist visas to travel to other Southeast Asian nations, you'll need to bring a couple extra passport-sized photos with you.

There are several ATMs in Bali that operate on the standard networks, but it's a good idea to have some extra cash on hand in case the network goes down. Traveler's checks are a choice, but it's also a good idea to pack some US dollars that you may use in case your ATM card is hacked to withdraw cash for unexpected expenses. check for any damage, tearing,or marking on large denominations.

You could be required to present documentation of an onward flight if you are arriving in Denpasar with a one-way ticket. The immigration officer has the last say in this. Save yourself some effort and have a printed copy of the information for your upcoming flight.

5. Bringing electronic equipment to Bali
Considering that cafes and guesthouses offer free Wi-Fi, you might want to bring your smartphone, tablet, ebook reader, or even a laptop. If you decide to bring delicate

electrical equipment, be aware of how to protect it in a tropical setting.

The two-pronged, circular CEE7 power outlets used in Europe are also used in Indonesia. The current is 50 Hz/230 volts. You won't need a step-down power transformer unless you want to bring a hair dryer (don't!). USB device chargers for laptops, smartphones, and other USB-compatible devices should be able to manage the higher voltage without any assistance. A compact travel adapter (passive) may be required to switch the type of the socket in some locations, even though many hotels feature universal outlets that are compatible with a variety of wire types.

6. Additional Items to Take with You to Bali

Consider including the following in addition to the obvious items:

For eating locally grown fruit at the seashore, a little knife is ideal. There is no doubt that you should include this in your checked bag!

Bring a small padlock with you to secure cabinets and storage lockers if you're staying at a hostel.

When using public latrines, bring hand sanitizer and toilet paper.

If your neighbors happen to enjoy parties, bring earplugs or headphones.

Bring a reusable straw to avoid adding to Asia's plastic trash crisis while enjoying cocktails and coconuts.

Using mosquito repellent will help you avoid being bitten by insects that could transmit dengue disease.

Flashlight for unforeseen power outages and nighttime strolls on the beach.

Protect devices and valuables with plastic bags or waterproof cases.

9.2 Local Transportation Guide

Taxis: In Bali, using a taxi is a convenient option, particularly when commuting short distances or with luggage. At the airport, popular destinations, and accommodations, cabs are simple to locate. Prior to beginning your trip, make sure to use metered taxis or to bargain the fee. Bali's Blue Bird and Grab are two well-known cab services.

Applications for ride-hailing: Grab is a well-liked app in Bali. To set up your pickup and drop-off points and book a trip, download the Grab app to your smartphone. Depending on your taste and the number of passengers, it provides solutions for both cars and motorcycles.

Renting a motorbike is a typical way to travel in Bali because they are convenient and make navigating the traffic much easier.

Rental motorcycles are offered by numerous nearby businesses and rental companies. Always ride with a helmet on and make sure you have a current international driver's license. Keep an eye on your surroundings, drive carefully, and abide by the regulations of the road.

Several car rental businesses are available in Bali if you prefer to drive a vehicle. You may go more independently and at your own leisure on the island if you rent a car. Keep your driver's license on you, abide by the rules of the road, and pay attention to parking limitations.

Public Buses: In comparison to other forms of transportation, public buses are less frequent and widespread in Bali. However, there are a few public bus routes that connect mostly important towns and popular tourist destinations. Trans Sarbagita, one of the major bus companies, provides service to Denpasar, Kuta, Nusa Dua, and other areas.

Shuttle Buses: In Bali, a lot of hotels and resorts provide shuttle bus services for its visitors. These shuttles might be a practical method to see the island as they frequently run between well-liked tourist spots. Ask your lodging about the availability and times of the shuttle services.

Bemo: In Bali, bemo is a type of traditional public transportation that resembles a tiny minivan or a truck that has been modified. They have set itineraries and can be less expensive for short journeys. Most frequently encountered in Denpasar, bemos are used for local transportation.

Cycling and Walking: The smaller towns and tourist destinations on Bali are frequently walkable and compact. Exploring the nearby markets, attractions, and beach regions on foot can be enjoyable. Since renting bicycles for tourists is widely available, cycling is also very common.

In some places of Bali, traffic congestion can be a problem, so be sure to plan your routes in advance, especially when traveling large distances or during rush hour. You might also think about utilizing a navigation software like Google Maps to assist you in navigating the island's roadways.

When using any mode of transportation, always put your safety first and drive carefully.

9.3 Suggested Websites and Apps for Travel

Numerous travel-related apps and websites can be quite helpful when organizing a vacation to Bali. Following are some suggestions:

Skyscanner (Website and App): Skyscanner is a well-liked website and mobile app for comparing flights, locating the best offers, and reserving flights to Bali.

Villas, guesthouses, and distinctive stays are just a few of the places Bali residents can choose from on Airbnb (website and app). It's a fantastic resource for discovering genuine and inexpensive accommodations.

Booking.com (website and app): Offering a wide range of Bali hotels, resorts, and other lodging options, Booking.com is a dependable website and app. It is renowned for its reasonable costs and streamlined UI.

TripAdvisor (Website and App): TripAdvisor is a thorough travel website that provides reviews, suggestions, and ratings for lodging, attractions, dining, and more. It might be useful for making travel plans and learning about Bali's top attractions.

Google Maps is an indispensable program for getting about Bali. It offers precise driving instructions, up-to-the-minute traffic data, and recommendations for nearby eateries, sightseers, and other sites of interest.

Go-Jek (App): In Bali, Go-Jek is a well-liked ride-hailing app. You can reserve vehicles, motorcycle taxis (often referred to as "ojeks"), and other types of transportation through it. It's practical and frequently less expensive than typical cabs.

A dependable software for currency conversion is XE Currency (app). It can assist you in controlling your spending in Bali by keeping you informed of the most recent exchange rates and allowing you to make wise selections.

If you're seeking distinctive dining opportunities in Bali, Eatwith is a great website. Travelers can meet local hosts who provide genuine meals and gourmet experiences through this service.

Klook is a platform for booking tours, activities, and attractions in Bali. It has a website with an app. It provides a wide variety of alternatives, including swimming, visiting temples, taking cooking classes, and more.

Bali.com (Website): Bali.com is an online travel guide for Bali that offers details on activities, lodging, tours, and cultural insights. It might be a useful tool when organizing your trip.

Prioritize your safety while traveling and always check the most recent travel advisories and local laws.

SUSTAINABLE TOURISM PRACTICES

Bali, a destination renowned for its stunning natural surroundings and diverse cultural legacy, has aggressively promoted sustainable tourism strategies to protect both its environment and its culture. Here are a few sustainable tourism strategies being used in Bali:

Bali has been taking measures to protect its natural resources, such as its beaches, forests, and marine habitats. The production of waste is being reduced, recycling is being encouraged, and less single-use plastic is being used. Efforts are made to maintain and restore coral reefs, and beach clean-up campaigns are periodically organized to keep the beaches tidy.

Responsible Water Management: Bali has a problem with water scarcity, especially in the dry season. Sustainable tourism strategies put an emphasis on prudent water management to address this. Hotels and resorts have put into place water-saving techniques include installing water-efficient fixtures, encouraging visitors to reuse towels and bed linens, and promoting sensible water consumption among tourists.

Engagement of Local people: Sustainable tourism in Bali attempts to involve local people and advance their welfare. There are initiatives to include locals in tourism-related activities, giving them access to employment possibilities and a fair part of the financial rewards. By promoting traditional art forms, handicrafts, and local enterprises, community-based tourism projects provide tourists a direct glimpse into the local way of life.

Cultural Preservation: Bali's distinctive cultural history is a major draw for travelers. Preservation and promotion of the island's indigenous arts, music, dance, and rituals are the main goals of sustainable tourism practices. Visitors are urged to observe local customs and traditions while visiting cultural sites and heritage villages, which are preserved and protected.

Eco-friendly Accommodations: To reduce their environmental impact, Bali's hotels and resorts have adopted a number of eco-friendly methods. This entails utilizing renewable energy sources, putting in place energy-efficient technologies, using less water, and properly managing waste. Even some lodgings use recycled and locally sourced materials in their construction, which complies with sustainable building norms.

Education and Awareness: Sustainable tourism methods in Bali place a strong emphasis on informing visitors about the value of ethical and environmentally friendly travel. Local initiatives and groups run awareness campaigns, workshops, and educational programs to advance responsible tourism, cultural sensitivity, and environmental preservation.

Ecotourism and nature-based activities: Bali has a wide range of ecotourism and nature-based activity alternatives. Visitor activities include exploring national parks, guided hikes, birdwatching, and wildlife conservation initiatives. These initiatives support the development of sustainable human-nature relationships and increase awareness of the significance of biodiversity protection.

It's significant to remember that despite Bali's progress in implementing sustainable tourism practices, there are still difficulties to be resolved. The government, local residents, and tourists themselves must work together constantly to strike a balance between the demands of tourism development and environmental and cultural preservation.

CONCLUSION

Bali is an alluring and varied travel destination that presents a special fusion of unspoiled natural beauty, rich culture, and gracious hospitality. Bali has grown to be a well-liked destination for tourists looking for a tropical paradise because of its gorgeous beaches, beautiful rice terraces, vivid temples, and dynamic arts scene.

The natural features of the island, which include well-known locations like Mount Agung and Mount Batur, offer stunning views and opportunities for outdoor pursuits including hiking, surfing, and diving. As a refuge for snorkeling and scuba diving aficionados and a window into the lively undersea world, Bali is known for its beautiful coral reefs.

Bali's cultural legacy is strongly influenced by Balinese Hinduism, as evidenced by the island's numerous temples, ceremonial rituals, and traditional arts and crafts. Visitors can fully experience the local culture by taking part in religious rites, watching mesmerizing dance performances, and visiting traditional marketplaces and art galleries.

There are a variety of lodging options on the island, from pricey resorts to affordable guesthouses, so there is something to meet any traveler's preferences and price range. The gastronomic scene in Bali is equally varied, with a vast range of regional specialties and foreign cuisine offered in restaurants and food carts all around the island.

Even though Bali has seen a rise in tourism recently, it has managed to hold onto its charm and attraction, with pockets of peace and unspoiled beauty still being discovered among the busy tourist spots. The island does, however, suffer several difficulties, including problems with waste management, excessive development in some regions, and environmental sustainability.

In general, Bali is still an alluring location that provides a variety of natural marvels, cultural activities, and friendly hospitality. Bali has something to offer everyone, whether they are looking for tranquility on pristine beaches, adventure in nature, or an introduction to a dynamic and varied culture.

Printed in Great Britain
by Amazon